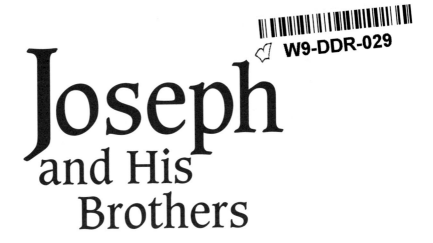

W9-DDR-029

Joseph
and His
Brothers

Cover illustration by
Michael Jaroszko

Story adaptation by
Sarah Toast

Interior illustrations by
Gary Torrisi

Interior art consultation by
David M. Howard, Jr., Ph.D.

Louis Weber, C.E.O.
Publications International, Ltd.
7373 North Cicero Avenue
Lincolnwood, Illinois 60646

Manufactured in U.S.A.

8 7 6 5 4 3 2 1

ISBN: 0-7853-2221-3

PUBLICATIONS INTERNATIONAL, LTD.
Rainbow is a trademark of Publications International, Ltd.

Long ago in Canaan, there lived a man named Jacob. Jacob was the father of twelve sons. And of his sons, he loved Joseph best of all. Jacob gave Joseph a richly colored coat with long sleeves, the kind that only an eldest son would wear.

But Joseph was not the eldest son. He had ten older brothers. When the older brothers saw Joseph in the special coat, they were very hurt and jealous.

Joseph made things worse by telling them his dreams. His dreams showed that someday his brothers would bow down to him.

Jacob's older sons took care of all the sheep. One day Jacob became worried when the sons had been away for a long time pasturing the sheep. He sent Joseph out to find them.

The brothers could see Joseph in his colorful coat from far away. All but one brother wanted to kill him. Reuben, the oldest, convinced the others into throwing Joseph down a dry well instead. He was planning to rescue Joseph later.

When Joseph reached his brothers, they tore off his coat and then threw him into the pit.

Reuben walked away, and the other brothers sat down to eat. After a while, a long line of traders passed by on their way to Egypt.

The brothers came up with a plan. They would sell Joseph to the traders for silver. Then Joseph would live, and they would have money.

The brothers pulled Joseph out of the pit and sold him. Then they killed a goat and smeared its blood over Joseph's coat. When they brought the coat to Jacob, he wept bitter tears. He thought Joseph had been killed by wild animals.

When the traders reached Egypt, they went to the slave market to sell Joseph to Potiphar, captain of the pharaoh's guard.

The Lord helped Joseph to do a good job for Potiphar. In time, Potiphar put Joseph in charge of his whole household.

All went well until Potiphar's wife blamed Joseph for something he hadn't done. Potiphar threw Joseph in prison.

Joseph was helpful in the prison. One day, he helped an important new prisoner, Pharaoh's cupbearer. Joseph explained that the cupbearer's dream meant that Pharaoh would forgive him.

Two years later, while Joseph was still in prison, the pharaoh had two troubling dreams that no one was able to explain. The cupbearer remembered how Joseph had once explained his dream.

The pharaoh sent for Joseph and told him of how he had dreamed that seven thin cows ate seven fat cows. He also told his dream of seven ears of withered grain eating seven full ears.

God helped Joseph explain that there would be seven years of rich harvests in Egypt followed by seven years in which nothing would grow.

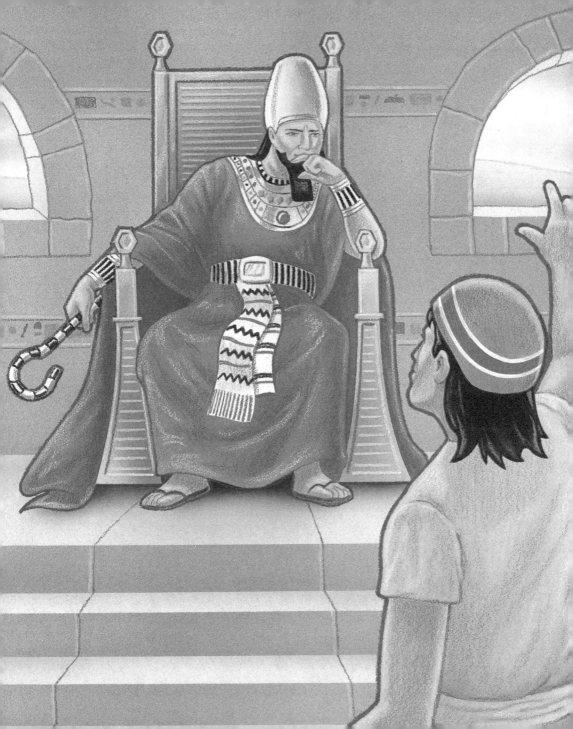

Joseph told Pharaoh to find a wise man to set aside food during the seven years of plenty so that in the seven years of want there would be plenty of food for everyone. God had given Joseph great wisdom, so the pharaoh decided to put Joseph in charge of the plan.

Joseph became the prime minister of Egypt. He was second only to Pharaoh. During the next seven years, Joseph saw that grain was stored in huge buildings. Then, during the seven years when no crops would grow, the people of Egypt could buy grain from Joseph.

In Canaan, Jacob's family needed food. Jacob sent ten of his sons to Egypt to buy grain. He kept the youngest son, Benjamin, at home.

When Joseph's ten older brothers came to buy grain, they bowed down before him. They didn't recognize him, but Joseph knew who they were.

Joseph wanted to find out whether they were still cruel and greedy. He sent all but one home with the grain. Their money was put back in the grain sacks. Joseph kept Simeon in prison until the others returned with Benjamin.

On the way back home, the brothers discovered they still had their money. When the grain was all eaten, Jacob let Benjamin go with the others to buy more grain in Egypt. They took along enough money to pay not only for the new grain but also to pay for the grain they had already bought.

Joseph sold his brothers more grain, but he had his servants put their money in the sacks as before. They also put Joseph's silver cup in Benjamin's sack.

Just outside the city, guards found Joseph's silver cup in Benjamin's sack.

The brothers were all taken back to Joseph. They fell down to the ground and begged to be let go.

Joseph agreed to let all of them go except Benjamin. At this, Judah said he would stay instead of Benjamin.

Joseph now knew that his brothers had become better men. He said, "I am your brother whom you sold into Egypt."

Then Joseph forgave them. "It was not you who sent me here; it was God. He sent me to keep many people alive."

Joseph hugged Benjamin and wept. Then he kissed all his brothers.

Pharaoh told Joseph to move his whole family from Canaan to Egypt. They were given the best grazing land.

At first, Jacob could not believe that his favorite son was still alive. But when they arrived in Egypt, Joseph greeted his family. The two men hugged and wept with happiness.